CHARLESTON
Food Crawls

CHARLESTON
Food Crawls

Jesse Blanco

TOURING *the* **NEIGHBORHOODS**
ONE BITE & LIBATION *at a* **TIME**

Globe
Pequot

ESSEX, CONNECTICUT

Globe Pequot

An imprint of Globe Pequot, the trade division of
The Rowman & Littlefield Publishing Group, Inc.
4501 Forbes Blvd., Ste. 200
Lanham, MD 20706
www.rowman.com

Distributed by NATIONAL BOOK NETWORK

Copyright © 2024 by Jesse Blanco

Maps by Melissa Baker © The Rowman & Littlefield Publishing Group, Inc.

Cover photo credits: top left: Tattooed Moose; top center: Lewis BBQ;
top right: Carmella's Desserts; middle right: Xiao Bao Biscuit; center left:
Jesse Blanco; bottom left: Jesse Blanco; center bottom: Explore Charleston; bottom right: Jesse Blanco

British Library Cataloguing in Publication Information available

Library of Congress Cataloging-in-Publication Data

Names: Blanco, Jesse, author.
Title: Charleston food crawls : touring the neighborhoods one bite &
    libation at a time / Jesse Blanco.
Description: Essex, CT : Globe Pequot, 2024 | Includes index.
Identifiers: LCCN 2023041178 (print) | LCCN 2023041179 (ebook) |
    ISBN 9781493058945 (paperback) | ISBN 9781493058952 (epub)
Subjects: LCSH: Restaurants—South Carolina—Charleston—Guidebooks. |
    Bars (Drinking establishments)—South Carolina—Charleston—
    Guidebooks. | Charleston (S.C.)—Guidebooks.
Classification: LCC TX907.3.S6732 C433 2024 (print) | LCC TX907.3.S6732
    (ebook) | DDC 647.95/757915—dc23/eng/20231002
LC record available at https://lccn.loc.gov/2023041178
LC ebook record available at https://lccn.loc.gov/2023041178

Printed in India

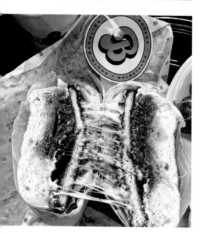

Contents

INTRODUCTION viii

FOLLOW THE ICONS ix

THE UPPER PENINSULA
THE YOU-WILL-NEED-A-CAR-FOR-THIS-CRAWL CRAWL 1

NORTH CENTRAL CHARLESTON
THE "KING STREET FOR LOCALS" CRAWL 13

SPRING STREET
THE HEART OF CHARLESTON'S BEST CULINARY NEIGHBORHOOD 25

UPPER KING STREET
THE ENTERTAINMENT AND DINING HUB 37

LOWER KING STREET
THE BEST SHOPPING STRETCH AND SOME GREAT EATS TOO 51

CITY MARKET AREA
THE CITY'S TOURIST HUB CRAWL 65

BAY STREET
OUR MOST UNDERRATED CRAWL 81

BROAD STREET
CHARLESTON'S ORIGINAL MAIN STREET CRAWL 95

PARC CIRCLE
A MODERN CULINARY SUBURB 109

THE "BEST OF THE REST" APPENDIX 121

ROOFTOP APPENDIX 123

PHOTO CREDITS 125

INDEX 127

ACKNOWLEDGMENTS 129

ABOUT THE AUTHOR 131

Introduction

On the night of April 4, 1998, I was given probably the best travel tip I had gotten to that point in my life and very likely since. It was my wedding night. The party was winding down and I found myself, just by happenstance, standing next to one of my dearest friends, Adria Valdesuso.

Adria was a former flight attendant for Pan Am. Remember them? She'd seen far more of the world than I had by the age of thirty. That included a six-month experience in Paris, the site of my honeymoon. Which at that point, was about twelve hours away from my arrival.

"What's your final advice for me going into Paris?" I asked.

"That's easy. Don't try to see it all in a week, because you won't and you will exhaust yourself trying. Just enjoy what you do get to see and eat. If you want to stop for coffee or a taste? Do it and enjoy it."

I cannot tell you how many times Adria's voice crossed my mind as I researched and prepared for this book during the winter of 2022–23.

Charleston, South Carolina's food scene easily ranks among the tops in the country. In the American South, it's a three-horse race for number 1, at least from my seat, the other two being New Orleans and Nashville. The grand irony there is that Miami could figure in the dialogue, but despite its location, I'd give Miami a separate distinction. There is nothing really "Southern" about South Florida. If you know what I mean.

Charleston, however? That's a different story altogether. Our nation's culinary history can be traced back to the Coastal South and the influences that arrived from Europe once upon a time. So much of what you can eat in Charleston can be traced to those dishes and influences. They are the foundation upon which an entire food scene rests.

Add in modern influences from chefs near and far and you have a beautiful melting pot of flavors in the Carolina Low Country. With more than 700 eateries squeezed into roughly 5 square miles that make up the Charleston Peninsula, you get the idea.

Just don't try to eat it all at once. Enjoy the ride—or in this case—the crawl.

Follow the Icons

 If you eat something outrageous and don't take a photo for Instagram, did you really eat it? These restaurants feature dishes that are Instagram famous. These foods must be seen (and snapped) to be believed, and luckily, they taste as good as they look!

 This icon means that sweet treats are ahead. Bring your sweet tooth to these spots for dessert first (or second or third).

 Cheers to a fabulous night out in Charleston! These spots add a little glam to your grub and are perfect for marking a special occasion.

 Follow this icon when you're crawling for cocktails. This symbol points out the establishments that are best known for their great drinks. The food never fails here, but be sure to come thirsty too!

THE UPPER PENINSULA CRAWL

1. **RANCHO LEWIS/EDMUND'S OAST BREWING COMPANY,** 1503 KING STREET, CHARLESTON, (843) 996-4500, RANCHOLEWISCHS.COM & EDMUNDSOAST.COM

2. **GOAT SHEEP COW, NORTH,** 804 MEETING STREET, CHARLESTON, (843) 203-3118, GOATSHEEPCOW.COM

3. **HOME TEAM BBQ,** 126 WILLIMAN STREET, CHARLESTON, (843) 225-7427, HOMETEAMBBQ.COM

4. **LEWIS BBQ,** 464 NASSAU STREET, CHARLESTON, (843) 805-9500, LEWISBARBECUE.COM

5. **THE ROYAL AMERICAN,** 970 MORRISON DRIVE, CHARLESTON, (843) 817-6925, THEROYALAMERICAN.COM

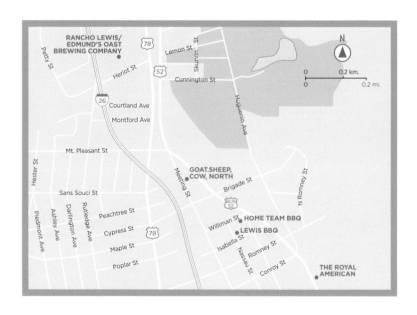

The Upper Peninsula

The You-Will-Need-a-Car-for-This-Crawl Crawl

You could ask a handful of locals what to call this particular section of Charleston and you would likely get a handful of answers. I did. The most common response was the Upper Peninsula. From the heart of this section of town, you are not more than 4 miles away from the Southern tip of the Charleston Peninsula. Still, you are very much a world away. Largely industrial with Interstate 26 running through a section of it, this Upper Peninsula is home to some of the best eats and sips in the region, making it impossible to overlook. Dotted with breweries and eateries we don't mention, it is also home to the eatery that got the most votes for the "where do F&B employees eat before or after work?" By far. We will get to that shortly.

From one end of this crawl to the other is just over 1 mile. Still, very little of it is foot-friendly. Making the use of a vehicle is imperative to enjoy the goods.

1

RANCHO LEWIS/EDMOND'S
OAST BREWING COMPANY

We chose to combine these two locations into one stop and a good a place to begin your crawl because they sit across a tiny courtyard from each other. They have different owners and are very different experiences, but they complement each other perfectly.

RANCHO LEWIS is the Tex-Mex spinoff of the highly popular Lewis BBQ family, which we'll dig into shortly.

What makes Rancho Lewis unique is his approach to "Fine Mexican food." You see, Lewis grew up in El Paso, Texas, where the flavors of Mexico are a unique blend of Texas, of course, but also Chihuahua, Mexico, and New Mexico, home of the world-famous Hatch chilies.

Lunch here was delicious and eerily reminiscent of my time as a news anchor along the Borderland of West Texas. There are some great eats out there, but you don't have to travel nearly that far. Lunch specials here are common, including fajitas and a fresh grab-them-yourselves salsa bar. Freshness is key here. In the food and those margaritas.

Across the way is **EDMONDS OAST BREWING COMPANY**. A large brewery and beer hall with some outdoor seating, it is home to roughly three dozen different beers. Some hang around, some rotate out. Either way, this stop is worth your time if you love sipping new brews.

2

GOAT SHEEP COW, NORTH

On the other end of the spectrum from beers and Mexican you will find our next stop. Of course, I am referring very literally to wine and cheese. **GOAT SHEEP COW, NORTH** is a sister cheese shop to the very popular Goat Sheep Cow in Charleston's South of Broad neighborhood.

I liked this spot for their selection of wines, some by the glass and many more available retail. The selection of cheeses was large enough to see the investment in variety here. The cheese connoisseur will enjoy this space complete with a café on one side providing pastries, coffees, or maybe something stronger. Owners Patty Floersheimer and Trudi Wagner will tell you their concept was developed to enjoy time with friends and a great bottle of wine. If that is your speed, this is your spot. I could spend an afternoon here. But we have crawling to do.

3 HOME TEAM BBQ

The BBQ game in Charleston sparks debate. Everyone has a favorite and really none of them are wrong. Generally, we don't traffic in chain restaurants in our travels, but there have been times when we make an exception. This is one of them. We do so because **HOME TEAM BBQ** started humbly right here in Charleston. They now have six locations across South Carolina and one in Aspen, Colorado. This one is their largest. I wish I could tell you the ribs are where it's at here, but I'm a sucker for the brisket. The chicken wings are incredibly popular, as is the rest of it. Six house made sauces at any given time only enhance the experience. You will not go wrong here.

4

LEWIS BBQ

What does it tell you when two of the best BBQ joints in town are located less than a block away from each other? There is a third, but we will get to that in a later crawl. For now, **LEWIS BBQ** is the parent restaurant of the Rancho Lewis concept that was our first stop on this crawl. John Lewis is a Central Texas trained pit master. That said, the locals will all steer you toward his brisket and it is special and their most popular. Their menu includes turkey breasts, pork ribs and sausage. If you've spent any time in Texas, then you get it. This is legit Texas BBQ right here in Charleston. A couple of sandwiches and an array of sides will leave you licking your fingers. If you are into that sort of thing, of course.

SAVE A FEW BUCKS!

Lewis BBQ is traditional Texas BBQ in the sense that they will sell you their meats by the pound, however much you want. If there are two of you, order a little more one time and share it from their tray. You are less likely to order too much that way. It's delicious but it is very rich and filling.

5

THE ROYAL AMERICAN

Our last stop on this crawl is the answer to the trivia question we shared with you during the introduction to this crawl. I polled no fewer than 10-12 F&B industry guys and gals during my research for this book. It wasn't unanimous, but it was close to it. "Where do you grab lunch before work or a late night bite after a shift?" THE ROYAL AMERICAN.

Located roughly a few miles away from the heart of tourist central on the Charleston Peninsula where so many of them make a living, the first choice for a bite "on the way in" or "on the way out" of downtown Charleston would appear to be the very popular Royal American.

Built into a 1950s-era iron forge, the Royal American prides itself on its old-school vibe. Or as they like to put it, Charleston's "gritty past."

Burgers are the go-to here, but anyone will tell you it is all great. Soups, apps, and more. Plus a full cocktail menu.

It is great food and open for lunch—and frankly, the closer you get into the heart of the peninsula, the harder it is to find that combination. Charleston's best eats are a 5 to 10 p.m. proposition. That doesn't mean you can't find great food at lunch, if you know where to go.

By night, the Royal American is a very popular live music venue, which also makes it a draw for locals. With plenty of seating indoor and outdoor.

THE NORTH CENTRAL CHARLESTON CRAWL

1. **RODNEY SCOTT'S WHOLE HOG BBQ,** 1011 KING STREET, CHARLESTON, (843) 990-9535, RODNEYSCOTTSBBQ.COM

2. **LITTLE JACK'S TAVERN,** 710 KING STREET, CHARLESTON, (843) 531-6868, LITTLEJACKSTAVERN.COM

3. **LEON'S,** 698 KING STREET, CHARLESTON, (843) 531-6500, LEONSOYSTERSHOP.COM

4. **RECOVERY ROOM TAVERN,** 685 KING STREET, CHARLESTON, (843) 727-0999, RECOVERYROOMTAVERN.COM

5. **NEON TIGER,** 654 KING STREET, CHARLESTON, (843) 640-3902, NEONTIGER.COM

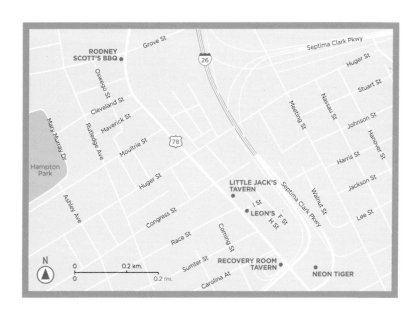

North Central Charleston

The "King Street for Locals" Crawl

Located not quite as far north as the Upper Peninsula section, but still not close enough into downtown Charleston to be given a more common designation, we classified this stretch of King Street as North Central. It is our introduction to Charleston's primary food and beverage artery into the peninsula—King Street. Along this stretch you will find more of a residential neighborhood than other stretches of King Street, which make it a comfortable walk. As you make your way less than 1 mile from one end of the crawl to the other, you will begin to see and feel the density of this city's food scene.

1

RODNEY SCOTT'S WHOLE HOG BBQ

At the end of the Upper Peninsula Crawl, we stopped at two of Charleston's best BBQ joints. At the time, I told you there would be a third. This is it. **RODNEY SCOTT'S BBQ**. There may be others out there that are very good, but along with the two we mentioned early, Rodney makes up the holy trinity of BBQ in Charleston.

You see, we buried the lede. Rodney Scott is a James Beard Award–winning BBQ Master (this country's highest culinary honor). Rodney's BBQ has been some of the most popular in the state for over a decade since his early days at a tiny crossroads in Hemmingway, South Carolina. Back in the day when people would drive hundreds of miles to line up for his unique spin on whole hog BBQ.

Since those simple beginnings, it would be easy to say Rodney has gone big time, with multiple locations around the South, including this flagship in Charleston. Rodney cuts no corners. This is high quality whole hog coal-fired BBQ. Which makes it different than the others we've mentioned but no less exceptional.

The Whole Hog Pork Sandwich and/or plate should be your first stop here. It's what made Rodney a star in the BBQ world. That said, I've never had anything on this menu that I didn't love. You will too. Rodney's is a must stop when you are in Charleston.

Great use of your time.

A walk through Charleston's North Central neighborhood gives you a good look at a neighborhood in transition. Gentrification is alive and well in this part of town. However, because of the distance between the beginning of this tour and the end, it might be worth considering bringing your car along between stops 1 and 2 before enjoying the rest of it on foot.

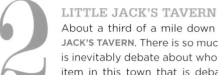

2 LITTLE JACK'S TAVERN

About a third of a mile down King Street you will find **LITTLE JACK'S TAVERN**. There is so much great food in Charleston, there is inevitably debate about who makes the best this or that. One item in this town that is debated, but not as much as other things, is the burger. The burger here at Little Jack's Tavern made them stars and they remain so today.

The Tavern Burger is your primary reason for a visit to Little Jack's, but certainly not the only one. Smallish and on the dark side, this space has a classic feel with a simple well-executed menu. The garlic and herb fries are a must, if that is your thing. If it isn't and a plate of them pass you, you might change your mind.

The margarita was among the best I've had in a decade. Simple and perfect. I'd order one 10 out of 10 visits there. Bon Appétit named Little Jack's among their best new restaurants in 2017. For a "Classic American Tavern," Little Jack's is what dreams are made of.

3

LEON'S

As you make your way a couple of blocks further down King Street toward our next stop, you will notice Melfi's Italian Restaurant across the street. Only open for dinner, it is regarded as one of the better Italian eateries in Charleston. Something to keep in mind. A block or so further down, you find our next stop, Leon's.

LEON'S OYSTER SHOP is maybe Charleston's most popular seafood and fried chicken "shack." It absolutely is with the locals, at any rate. When asked what for Charleston's most popular spot to begin a Sunday Funday, one bartender immediately responded, "Oh that's easy, Leon's."

Wonderfully inviting and absolutely family friendly, Leon's is known for a number of things, including their "world famous" grilled oysters. Fried chicken and fry baskets featuring shrimp, catfish, clams, or oysters are very popular as well. There is a good selection of sandwiches, salads and sides, but the oysters and chicken are top on the list.

As you might imagine, their rosé or gin and tonic slushees are popular in the warmer months with the day drinking crowd. The scene just feels like the kind of place you would love to visit after a long day at the beach (if only the nearest beach was less than a half hour away). Cold beer, salty food, and a great vibe.

4 THE RECOVERY ROOM

A couple of so blocks further down King Street, you will see the overpass ahead that is an unofficial border between where we are and Upper King Street, which is another crawl altogether later on. It's a good one too.

Before you get to the overpass on the right across King Street, you will find an old house with a sign on it that says "**THE RECOVERY ROOM.**"

"The Rec Room" as, it is known to locals, is a pretty straight-forward dive bar and restaurant. During the week they open at 2 p.m. On the weekends, noon. Those two factors make them fair game in my book. Sometimes you just want some great wings or a burger. As dive bar food goes, this is great. The later it gets in the evening, the greater it is, right? Seriously though, this is solid food with enjoyable seating outdoors, if that's your thing, and a full liquor bar (duh).

By night, this is one of local Charleston's gathering spots to dance the night away before you Uber home.

5 NEON TIGER

This is probably the biggest departure from one stop to the next on any crawl we share with you. Standing in front of the Recovery Room Tavern continuing under the overpass and on the left is one of Charleston's rock star vegan restaurants, **NEON TIGER**.

They open at 5 p.m., so unless it is later in the day, there isn't a need to walk down there.

They bill themselves as "proudly local, dimly lit and wholly vegan" (and it is). This is a Big City vibe through and through. Oh, and the food is excellent! If there is a vegan in your group, this should be looked into.

HISTORY RIGHT BEFORE YOUR EYES: JUST BEYOND THE HIGH-WAY OVERPASS, YOU WILL FIND LINE STREET. THERE ARE NO HISTORIC MARKERS, THERE ARE NO ARTIFACTS. BUT THIS AREA WAS NAMED FOR A FORTIFICATION DURING THE WAR OF 1812. LIKELY A NORTHERN EXTREME OF THE CITY AT THE TIME.

THE SPRING STREET CRAWL

1. **XIAO BAO BISCUIT,** 224 RUTLEDGE AVENUE, CHARLESTON, XIAOBAOBISCUIT.COM

2. **PINK CACTUS,** 100A SPRING STREET, CHARLESTON, (843) 764-9343, PINKCACTUS.COM

3. **THE PASS,** 207-A ST. PHILIP STREET, CHARLESTON, (843) 444-3960, THEPASSCHS.COM

4. **MALAGÓN,** 33 SPRING STREET, CHARLESTON, (843) 926-0475, MALAGONCHS.COM

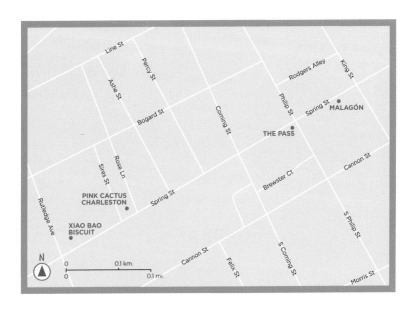

Spring Street

The Heart of Charleston's Best Culinary Neighborhood

This neighborhood is so rich and overflowing with not just good eats but great eats, it was originally going to be two crawls. Under the right circumstances, we could probably make three or maybe four. Ultimately, the fact that so many of the great restaurants in this Cannonborough/Elliotborough neighborhood only offer dinner service, it makes it a little different to offer a crawl during the dinner hour at these places. Instead, I found that most of the best midday eats in this area line the street that runs straight through the heart of it: Spring Street.

You could spend an entire weekend in just this neighborhood and not eat all of the great food surrounding you. Good problems to have, right? We can try though.

1

XIAO BAO BISCUIT

A little over a decade ago, this old-time service station converted into a restaurant opened with an Asian concept. Modern spins on some Asian classics. People couldn't get enough of it. It was the talk of the town for quite some time. It was fresh, it was casual, and it was absolutely delicious. The good news for us is that it remains all of those things. Dumplings (fried or steamed), noodles or rice bowls, you name it. There is really nothing on this menu we haven't loved. The go-to here (their most popular) is the Okonomiyaki—a Japanese crispy cabbage pancake topped with sweet soy, furikake mayo, and chili garlic sauce. If you are hungry, add some protein in the form of an egg or bacon or pork belly. It's a show-stopper.

2

PINK CACTUS MEXICAN

Making your way east up Spring Street, you find a beautiful and relatively quiet main drag in this neighborhood lined with galleries, flower shops, and other businesses. Two short blocks up, you reach our next stop in a tiny strip mall: **PINK CACTUS**.

Fair to say there are quite a few good Mexican eats in Charleston, these are some of them. They are open all day, which helps. The scene here at Pink Taco is far more energetic at night, but that won't stop us from popping in for a quick bite or a margarita during our crawl.

They offer a daily lunch special, which varies, but it usually includes a glass of Hibiscus or other floral water. We've enjoyed the carnitas here. The guac as well. Pink Cactus shouldn't be overlooked.

> TAKE IN THE NEIGHBORHOOD! ONLY A FRACTION OF WHAT THERE IS TO SEE IN THIS CANNONBOROUGH/ELLIOTBOROUGH NEIGHBORHOOD IS ALONG SPRING STREET. DON'T BE AFRAID TO WANDER UP A RESIDENTIAL SIDE STREET FOR A LOOK AT A NEIGHBORHOOD FULL OF ENERGY, YOUTH, AND PROGRESS. OLD HOMES, YES, BUT THE YOUTHFUL PASSION IS REFRESHING.

3

THE PASS SANDWICH SHOP

Leaving Baguette Magic and turning right, our next stop is a couple of blocks away with plenty to see between here and there.

One block up is the corner of Spring and Coming Streets. Around here, this qualifies as a major intersection downtown. Cars traveling up can reach high speeds when the lights are green, so be mindful of traffic. Also at that corner, you will look across Spring Street at a large white columned building. This is Charleston's Karpeles Manuscript Library Museums, one of roughly seventeen such museums across America.

Before crossing Coming Street, look to the right immediately down the street. A few feet ahead you will see the Tippling House, a nationally acclaimed spot for wine and light bites.

On to the sandwich shop! One block up at Spring and St. Philip Streets, you'll find **THE PASS, PANINO AND PROVISIONS**.

The Pass is a classic Italian sandwich shop and tiny market. With sandwiches named "Such a Nice Italian Boy" and Panino de Basilico (basil-lemon chicken salad!) you can easily see why they are so popular, because they are. There is some seating in here, though not a lot. I imagine seating could be tough to come by at peak lunchtime, although I'm gathering there is a ton of to-go going on here. I crave these sandwiches. You will too.

4 MALAGÓN

Crossing St. Philip Street and continuing up Spring, and about ⅔ of the way into the next block, you will find our final spot on this crawl: MALAGÓN MERCADO Y TAPERÍA.

I love this spot for a lot of reasons. Including the fact that it is open during the day and offers a comfortable and somewhat "higher end" dining experience than what we've been enjoying to this point.

Don't get me wrong, Malagón is very approachable and casual, but classic Spanish taperías can really be whatever you want them to be. Tapas are small plates made to share, a concept made very popular in Spain. High-quality cured meats and cheeses, plus full plates to include meats or seafood. Crusty breads and wine. Wine everywhere. Enough red wine to drown Barcelona . . . well, maybe. But you get the picture. The menu here ebbs and flows, as they do at a lot of true taperías. What is here tomorrow may not be next week. So there are no go-tos. Except all of it, which we enjoyed on multiple visits.

THE KARPELES MUSEUM IN CHARLESTON IS HOUSED IN A FORMER METHODIST CHURCH NAMED ST. JAMES CHAPEL, BUILT IN 1856. DURING THE CIVIL WAR, CONFEDERATES USED THE BUILDING AS A HOSPITAL AND STORED MEDICAL SUPPLIES THERE. IT IS OPEN TO THE PUBLIC WITH A REVOLVING SERIES OF OVER 1 MILLION DOCUMENTS ON EXHIBIT.

THE UPPER KING STREET CRAWL

1. **FÉLIX COCKTAILS ET CUISINE,** 550 KING STREET, CHARLESTON, (843) 203-6297, FELIXCHS.COM

2. **THE ORDINARY,** 544 KING STREET, CHARLESTON, (843) 414-7060, EATTHEORDINARY.COM

3. **CALLIE'S HOT LITTLE BISCUIT,** 476½ KING STREET, CHARLESTON, (843) 737-5159, CALLIESBISCUIT.COM

4. **BODEGA CHS,** 23 ANN STREET, CHARLESTON, 29403, (843) 297-4772, BODEGACHS.COM

5. **LA PÂTISSERIE AT THE BENNETT HOTEL,** 404 KING STREET, CHARLESTON, (843) 577-7562, HOTELBENNETT.COM

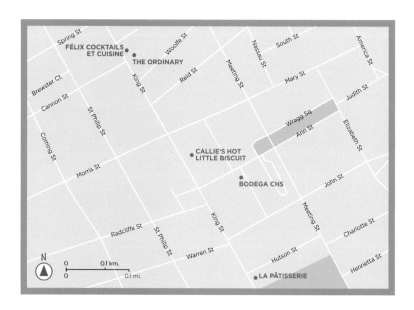

Upper King Street

The Entertainment and Dining Hub

This is, without question, Charleston's most densely populated stretch of food and drink. The number of spots worthy of a mention along this roughly 5-block stretch of Upper King Street could probably fill three crawls. As a general rule, if they are only open in the evening, we are keeping them off of our crawl, with the exception of one that we will explain. What does it say about this stretch when two of the better restaurants in all of the South sit at either end of it? One is a seafood restaurant, the other a chophouse.

In between you can find anything from beer halls targeting something of a younger demographic, to fancy rooftop bars, brunch, sweets, cocktails, Italian, Mexican, and more. If you see a spot along the stroll that appeals to you, go ahead and stop, enjoy the ride.

1

FÉLIX COCKTAILS ET CUISINE

When you have spent over a decade writing about food and drink, it is easy to fall out of the habit of naming favorites. I just don't do it. There is too much to enjoy for different reasons. That said, if I had to pick a spot I most enjoyed during multiple visits researching this book, it was FÉLIX.

Félix is a French-inspired eatery, an American Brasserie, if you will. The room is beautiful, the food is exceptional. Whatever you get, don't pass on the truffle fries. They are legendary around these parts, as is their espresso martini. Shots of espresso brewed right in front of you for every cocktail. The way it should be. The menu is fantastic. On Saturdays and Sundays they open at 10 a.m. for brunch. A perfect way to start a weekend.

2

THE ORDINARY

About 75 feet from the door to Félix sits one of the most renowned seafood spots in Charleston. It's been that way since they opened roughly a decade ago. Simply put, there is nothing ordinary about **THE ORDINARY**.

The Ordinary oyster hall, as they refer to themselves, is focused on their raw bar. It certainly isn't all they do (and they do it all well), but it can be a focus in this beautifully restored historic bank building.

The seafood towers, loaded with oysters, clams, shrimp, and more will get your attention. Acting on a tip, I went for one of their very popular crispy oyster sliders with Nuoc cham (Vietnamese dipping sauce) and fresno pepper mayo on a fresh-baked Hawaiian roll. It was one of best bites I enjoyed in three months visiting Charleston. I waited an hour for a seat to try that bite, and I would do it again tomorrow.

This is the only stop on this crawl that we mention that only opens for dinner service, generally at 5 p.m. Consider stopping for a quick bite and a glass of champagne as soon as they open before going off for a proper dinner somewhere else. Although a reservation here certainly wouldn't be a bad choice either.

2ND SUNDAYS

If you are feeling like there is a lot to take in along this stretch with limited room on the sidewalk to handle the crowds, you are not alone. That's part of why Charleston hosts 2nd Sundays every month. A half-mile stretch of "Upper King Street" (from Queen to Calhoun) is closed to vehicular traffic between noon and 5 p.m. This allows visitors to see the street as a whole with no cars or other interference and enjoy as they see fit. Visit charlestoncvb.com for more about 2nd Sundays.

3

CALLIE'S HOT LITTLE BISCUIT

Depending on the time of day, but particularly on a weekend night, this next stretch of 2 blocks or so of Upper King Street can make for some of the most intense people watching you will find in Charleston. As we mentioned, there is something for everyone along this very crowded stretch of the city. Two highlights would be Prohibition for their charred chicken wings and cocktail program and The Darling Oyster Bar with their family-friendly raw bar and seafood. Enjoy the walk.

A couple of blocks down you will come upon a Charleston classic: **CALLIE'S HOT LITTLE BISCUIT**. Pay attention. If you blink you will miss it. Unless, of course, you see the crowd pouring in or out.

Callie's biscuits are legendary and for good reason. They are delicious. Carrie Morey has literally turned this sliver of a storefront on Upper King Street into a biscuit empire. Two cookbooks and a PBS television series later, Callie's biscuits are such a draw she has two locations here in downtown Charleston, the other being inside the City Market.

Try one, try them all. They are small, but they are delicious. Then when you get hooked, because you just might, you can mail order them to your door year-round.

4 BODEGA CHS

Continuing South on King, our next stop will take us a few steps off of this main drag for the next hidden treasure. Before we veer off, however, I must point out Glazed Gourmet Doughnuts across King Street and roughly a half block down from where you left the biscuit shop. If you get there early enough, these doughnuts are wonderful! They are best when they are fresh, and they don't last long into the day.

The next street corner you will come to is the intersection of King and Ann Streets. Here we are going to cross Ann and make a left. Just ahead on the right you will find the Children's Museum of the Low Country. Just beyond that is a long brick-paved courtyard. Enter that courtyard and walk about 200 feet. On the left you will find a hidden gem that everyone knows about: **BODEGA**.

Bodega is a sandwich shop and bar. Breakfast sandwiches are big here, but the rest of it is popular as well. Why? Well, they are delicious. That part is assumed, right? Well, they are also huge. The variety is wonderful as well, including a fried green tomato sandwich. There are vegan options as well as cold sandwiches and hot. I visited here on a last-minute whim and I am very glad I did. They have a serious coffee program as well as a full liquor bar on the other side. Live music in the evenings as well.

TIP

Hall's Chophouse is as iconic as they come in this city. Family owned and operated since day one, Hall's is not only one of the best in Charleston but the South or the country for that matter. Lunch is available only on weekends. Tables are tough to come by. The bar area accepts walk-ins, but at happy hour you may have trouble squeezing in or hearing yourself think. Yes, it is that good.

5

LA PÂTISSERIE

Leaving Bodega and turning right back up to Ann Street, you will now turn left and continue back to King Street. At that corner, you will turn left and continue South along King Street.

Traveling down King you will come on one of the finest steakhouses in the South. Hall's Chophouse flagship location is as legendary as you may have heard it is. Simply wonderful and everything a classic steakhouse should be. Well worth a visit if you're around after 5 p.m. or for Sunday brunch. A couple of tiny city blocks ahead you will find our final stop.

LA PÂTISSERIE sits at the corner of King and Hutson Streets, but it is technically inside the Hotel Bennett. This is a classic French pastry shop. Its colorful case will likely offer you anything you'd find in St. Germain des Prés in Paris. It is an excellent choice.

If you are looking for something a little less fancy and more local, per-haps, you should consider Kudu Coffee and Craft Beer. It is everything a local coffee shop should be. Standing in front of La Pâtisserie, it is across King Street and about 200 feet down Vanderhorst Street. You can clearly see their sign from King Street.

THE LOWER KING STREET CRAWL

1. **CAVIAR & BANANAS GOURMET MARKET AND CAFÉ,** 51 GEORGE STREET, CHARLESTON, (843) 577-7757, CAVIARANDBANANAS.COM

2. **OFF TRACK ICE CREAM,** 6 BEAUFAIN STREET, CHARLESTON, OFFTRACKICECREAM.COM

3. **167 RAW OYSTER BAR,** 193 KING STREET, CHARLESTON, (843) 579-4997, 167RAW.COM

4. **CHOCOLAT BY ADAM TURONI,** 194 KING STREET, CHARLESTON, (843) 444-3945, CHOCOLATAT.COM

5. **BIN 152 WINE SHOP,** 152 KING STREET, CHARLESTON, (843) 577-7359, BIN152.COM

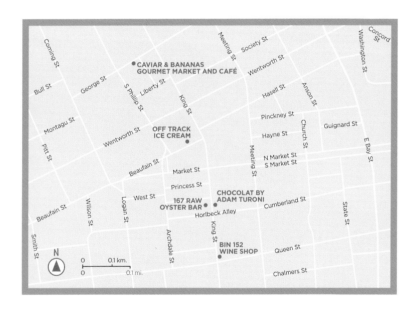

Lower King Street

The Best Shopping Stretch and
Some Great Eats Too

Having taken in the most certainly "higher octane" scene along Upper King Street in Charleston, you will find that Lower King is demonstrably quieter. Dramatically so. Why? The better part of Lower King (which begins at Marion Square on Calhoun Street) is dominated by retail. The best shopping in town, by the way. Which means they close up shop in the evening. There are very few late nights in this part of the city. The stretch is dotted, however, with great bites. Here are a few.

1
CAVIAR & BANANAS GOURMET MARKET AND CAFÉ

At the intersection of King and Calhoun Streets, we begin our walk south down a lovely tree-covered section of King Street. one of the few along this stretch. A lot of this walk will be in the sun, fast food and some local eateries sprinkled along the way. As we mentioned, lots of opportunities for shopping. They also begin almost immediately. At George Street we will turn right and walk up about ¼ block to our first stop, **CAVIAR & BANANAS**.

Located a stone's throw from the heart of the College of Charleston, Caviar & Bananas is a very popular breakfast and lunch spot for good reason.

Strange as the name may sound, their sandwiches are fresh, the baked goods are solid, and their coffee program is as consistent as any you will find in the neighborhood. There's a grab-and-go section as well as a great gelato selection. This is a refreshing stop on a warm summer day. When school is in session, you'll know it at lunchtime. You'll know it early, too, with students running through for their daily caffeine fix.

OFF TRACK ICE CREAM

If you exit Caviar and Bananas and turn left, you will almost immediately find yourself in the heart of the College of Charleston's campus, which you might enjoy for a stroll. Otherwise, returning to King Street and turning to the right to continue South, you will once again encounter a heavy dose of retail. Three or so blocks ahead, you will reach Beaufain Street. Turn to the right and proceed about 150 feet to our next stop, **OFF TRACK ICE CREAM**.

This is one of a very small handful of quality ice cream shops in Charleston. I love this one, because it is modern and inventive and most importantly—to me anyway—it is all made here, which makes this ridiculously delicious. Flavors like Tahitian Vanilla Bean and Cookies and Cream will satisfy the mainstream crowd. S'mores Pop Tart and Salted Pretzel Toffee get my attention. Not to mention a serious variety of vegan flavors, again made in house, with cashews and coconut cream. A real treat. Expect a line in the evening.

A STREET FIT FOR A KING

King Street is Charleston's second most historic street after Meeting Street. With a history dating back beyond three hundred years, King Street was Charleston's primary commercial street in and out of the city while most of the activity centered around the waterfront. It is named for King Charles II of England, for whom Charles Towne was also named.

3

RAW 167 OYSTER BAR

Back up to King Street, we turn to the right and continue down King to our next stop, which will be the most serious eats on the crawl as well as some of the most serious eats in the city. Three and a half tiny blocks ahead on the right you will reach **RAW 167 OYSTER BAR**.

If you consider yourself a raw bar aficionado, you'll want to plan your crawl around this stop. They do not accept reservations. Not at all. As such, tables can be very hard to come by, particularly on the weekends. It is Charleston's best raw bar that is open for lunch, which is a huge plus while crawling. I've never had anything I didn't love here. Don't pass on the espresso martini. It's a thing here.

4

CHOCOLAT BY ADAM TURONI

The good news about this stop is that you can pop in while waiting for your table at the raw bar directly across the street. It's a distance of about 75 feet.

ADAM TURONI is a Savannah-based chocolate maker who specializes in an overly impressive array of truffles and sweet nibbles. Every single bite is made by hand in Savannah. Popular bites include the Savannah Honey Chocolate Bar, the Raspberry Chambord Truffle, and

Soups up! This particular crawl ends near the intersection of King and Queen Streets. A few paces up Queen and you will arrive at 82 Queen, one of Charleston's more popular traditional Southern restaurants. It is a beautiful space, but they are known in large part for the she-crab soup. If you have room for it (and we all have room for soup, don't we?), it is worth a visit while sitting in their beautiful courtyard.

the Milk Chocolate Peanut Butter cups. There are plenty of others, and this shop is tiny so it's a quick browse. Take a few in a bag and enjoy them later. If you love chocolates, there is nothing here you will not absolutely love.

5

BIN 152 WINE SHOP

Back out on King Street, continue South you will continue to notice an abundance of boutiques, antiques, and other shopping. On the left, an ornate building with a stairway up to the front door is the Charleston Library Society—the third-oldest subscription library in America, founded in 1748. A few steps ahead on the same side of the street as the library is our final stop, Bin 152 Wine Shop.

BIN 152 bills itself as Charleston's oldest and most respected wine bar. What we can confirm is that it offers the largest selection of wines by the glass in the city. Roughly 40 choices by the glass, give or take, means there is something for everyone. After all the walking and shopping you've enjoyed on this stretch, a perfectly crisp white or rosé paired with one of Bin 152's signature charcuterie boards might be exactly what you need.

CHARLESTON CITY MARKET AREA CRAWL

1. **HYMAN'S SEAFOOD,** 215 MEETING STREET, CHARLESTON, (843) 723-6000, HYMANSSEAFOOD.COM

2. **BENNE'S BY PENINSULA GRILL,** 112 NORTH MARKET STREET, CHARLESTON, (843) 872-9833, BENNESCHARLESTON.COM

3. **CLERKS COFFEE AT HOTEL EMELINE,** 181 CHURCH STREET, CHARLESTON, 29401, HOTELEMELINE.COM

4. **CHURCH AND UNION,** 32B N. MARKET STREET, CHARLESTON, (843) 937-8666, CHURCHANDUNIONCHARLESTON.COM

5. **BYRD COOKIE COMPANY,** 71 S. MARKET STREET, CHARLESTON, (843) 492-6312, BYRDCOOKIECOMPANY.COM

6. **PORT OF CALL FOOD COURT AND BREW HALL,** 99 S. MARKET STREET, SUITE 5, CHARLESTON, (843) 473-4832, PORTOFCALLCHS.COM

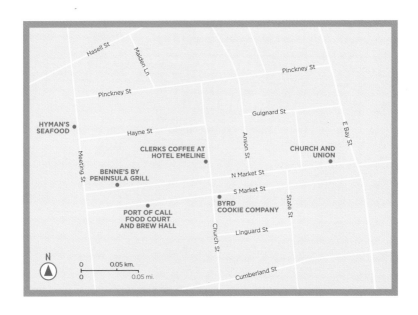

City Market Area

The City's Tourist Hub Crawl

Any city as old as Charleston is going to have a section of town that draws a majority of visitors in search of its historic relevance. This is generally the part of the city where you will find the largest collection of historic buildings, landmarks, and stories tied to its past. While there are historic landmarks scattered throughout the Charleston Peninsula, the heart of its background is tied to the general area known today as City Market.

The area is larger than the generic borders of North and South Market Streets. Down the middle is a 4-block Marketplace building featuring some food but primarily local arts and crafts. On either side you will find seemingly endless choices for food or drink targeting tourists. It can be overwhelming. While there are certainly more good choices to stop for a nosh than we list in this crawl, we think we've hit a few high notes for you to indulge.

1

HYMAN'S SEAFOOD

Our tour of the City Market area actually begins on Market Street and a seafood landmark.

HYMAN'S SEAFOOD is a Charleston institution, plain and simple. The seafood house and deli dates back to the 1890s. It only became Hyman's Seafood in 1987. Still, you don't last that long, of course, unless you are doing something well—in this case, giving visitors what they are looking for when they travel to a historic Southern city. Seafood and lots of it. Fried and otherwise.

The crowd outside is there year-round. There is always a wait for a seat. Inside, you are more likely to meet someone from your hometown than you will from Charleston. It is one of this town's most popular one-stop shops for a sampling of the flavors of the Carolina coast. Hushpuppies, she-crab soup, chowders, and more.

APPETIZERS

Carolina Delight – 11.95
Shrimp and grits taken up a notch!
Lightly fried grit cake topped
with your choice of shrimp,
salmon or salmon croquette.
Add cheese and bacon 3.95

Chilean Seabass Croquette – 10.00
Broiled only. Drizzled
with our secret sauce.

Wadmalaw Delight – 8.95
Local fried green tomatoes
served over creamy grits, topped
with Hyman's Parmesan cream
sauce and cheddar cheese

Shrimp or Salmon-a-Grits – 10.95
Shrimp or Salmon and creamy
grits topped with Hyman's
special Parmesan cream sauce
Add cheese and bacon 3.95

Boom Boom Shrimp – 11.95
Crispy shrimp tossed in sweet
and spicy sauce served over
fresh cut potato chips

Prince Edward Island Mussels – 11.95
Scampi style served with garlic bread

Chilled Shrimp
Fresh, Chilled Shrimp
seasoned with old bay
½ pound

Salmon Croquettes – 8.95
Made with 95% fresh salmon
topped with our secret sau

Fried Green T

2 BENNE'S BY PENINSULA GRILL

Exiting Hyman's Seafood directly across Meeting Street at the corner of Market and Meeting you find one of the most popular fine dining establishments in the city, **PENINSULA GRILL**.

Peninsula Grill is known for a lot of things. It's a beautiful, classic Southern dining room offering classic dishes in a gorgeous setting. While all the food is very good, it is their signature coconut cake that (according to *Southern Living* Magazine) is "the stuff of legend." And they are right. Fortunately for us, there is a new addition to the Peninsula Grill family that will allow you to enjoy that cake and more without sporting your Sunday best in a fine dining environment.

Directly adjacent to Peninsula Grill on North Market Street sits Benne's. A dessert bar and cocktail space that I'm guessing was built in large part to handle the demand for that practically world-famous coconut cake.

Have a slice and a cup of coffee. The latter is exceptional as well. That cake will leave you wanting more, or asking them to ship a whole cake home for you, which they can and will do. In a city full of delightful bites, this is a classic taste of heaven. You should not skip it.

3 CLERKS COFFEE COMPANY AT HOTEL EMELINE

Exiting Benne's, turn left and continue along North Market Street. There is so much to see here. Retail and more. If anything catches your eye, feel free to stop and enjoy. Then our crawl continues ahead to Church Street, where we will turn left and walk about 100 feet to **CLERKS COFFEE**.

Clerks is a favorite little oasis of mine, a fabulous spot to cool off for a few minutes (and maybe recharge one of your devices). The coffee and tea program is solid and the lavender lemonade is delicious and wonderfully refreshing on a hot Southern summer day. Looking for something with a bite? How about a lazier pear with pear vodka, spiced pear, and lemon.

This is also a good time to recommend Frannie and the Fox, the hotel's wonderful Italian concept for dinner. There's a beautiful courtyard and fireplace in the back; take a peek. The food is wonderful. One of my favorite Italian bites in town and also very popular with locals despite its location inside of the Hotel Emeline.

Given the popularity of the City Market section of Charleston, there's a common misconception of its origins. Many people incorrectly refer to this area as Slave Market. This is not accurate. Slaves were never sold here. They were sold on nearby wharves and other local markets such as Old Slave Mart on Chalmers Street, which is now a museum.

4

CHURCH AND UNION CHARLESTON

Exiting Clerks and walking back to North Market, we turn left and cross Church Street. Just ahead above eye level you will see one of Charleston's more casual rooftops at Henry's on the Market, which is good for a nosh and a view if that's your speed. Our next stop, however, is just ahead on the left. **CHURCH AND UNION CHARLESTON**.

I've been a fan of this space for a long time. When you walk in, you'll see why. Once upon a time, it was called 5Church. Once upon a longer time, this building was, in fact, a church.

Now, it is one of my favorite stops for a beverage. The scene speaks for itself (Sun Tzu's *The Art of War* is transcribed on the ceiling). And oh by the way, the food I've enjoyed here over the years has kept me coming back.

TIP

Buyer Beware! For all of the wonderful culinary delights you will find in this beautiful city, the City Market area is very tourist-centric and, as a result, not one of the best areas in town to enjoy a meal. Is there good food around here? Absolutely. Is there a higher concentration of overpriced tourist food around here? This is also true. Which, frankly, makes Charleston no different than any other city in the world with a high number of visitors.

5

BYRD COOKIE COMPANY

Exiting Church and Union, we cross North Market at Bay Street. At the eastern end of City Market on your left, we continue the short trip across a second street, South Market, for the return trip back down the other side of this City Market area. Again you will see plenty by way of tourist-centric eats and some shopping. Our next stop is two full blocks ahead . . . and they are waiting for you with a free sample.

BYRD COOKIE COMPANY is a national brand based in Savanah, Georgia. Charleston is far from the only place you will find them. They are available by mail nationwide and even on a couple of airlines. Why? Their Scotch oatmeal cookies are some of the best you will ever have. Try one.

Key lime or lemon coolers are delicious as are the more standard flavors like chocolate chip or shortbread. If you've never experienced Byrd cookies, you should. The recipe for those oatmeal cookies has been around for over 100 years. I can almost guarantee you, if you take some home, you will at some point mail order some more. They're highly addictive.

6 PORT OF CALL FOOD COURT AND BREW HALL

Continuing along South Market Street back toward Meeting Street, we once again cross Church Street and find our final stop in the middle of the next block, with a little bit of something for everyone.

On the left, you will find a tree-covered courtyard with a bar on one side. Behind it, a set of doors will give you access to a small food court. There are only four vendors in there, but it is worth a look. Street food is the name of the game in here, with food truck entrepreneurs setting up shop at this location for a short time to expand their business a little. Burgers, Greek, Mexican, you never know what you'll find.

You can take your food out to the court-yard and enjoy. Many times during the day there is live music. It's a fun stop for some quick inexpensive local eats.

THE BAY STREET CRAWL

1. **167 SUSHI,** 289 EAST BAY STREET, CHARLESTON, (843) 625-3031, 167RAW
    .COM

2. **BIG JOHN'S TAVERN,** 251 EAST BAY STREET, CHARLESTON, (843) 641-7269,
    ILOVEBJS.COM

3. **RUDY ROYALE,** 209 EAST BAY STREET, CHARLESTON, (843) 297-4443,
    RUDYROYALE.COM

4. **CARMELLA'S CAFÉ AND DESSERT BAR,** 198 EAST BAY STREET,
    CHARLESTON, (843) 722-5893, CARMELLASDESSERTBAR.COM

5. **THE GRIFFON,** 18 VENDUE RANGE, CHARLESTON, (843) 723-1700,
    GRIFFONCHARLESTON.COM

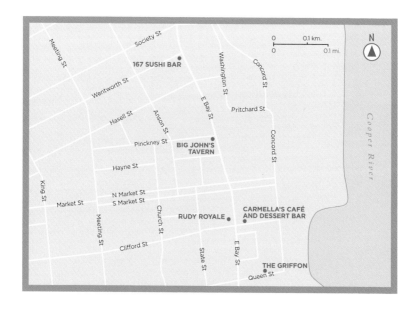

Bay Street

Our Most Underrated Crawl

While it would be easy to get caught up in all of the shiny objects you will find scattered all about on our other crawls, this one along East Bay Street probably features the best combination of food and drink plus historic sights and places you should see for that Instagram post. Of course, there are plenty of others, but this one is unique. You will soon see why.

To the north, East Bay Street runs past shipping docks and out of the city. To the south from our starting point, you will see Charleston's cruise ship port. But otherwise, as you make your way south, you will see more and more to see and do, culminating with either a beautiful waterfront peek at Charleston's famed Rainbow Row and/or its signature pineapple fountain. Both of which are less than 10 minutes apart by foot.

1

167 SUSHI BAR

On the Lower King Street crawl in this book we introduced you to 167 Raw, one of the more popular raw bar and seafood restaurants in town. That restaurant's original location was here at 289 Bay Street. When it moved to King, this space became one of the best spots for sushi in Charleston, **167 SUSHI**.

The quality of the fish here speaks for itself; the reputation of the 167 group as a provider of some of Charleston's freshest cuts ensures that you will have a quality sushi experience. Nigiri, sashimi, and futomaki dominate the menu, but you will also find poke bowls, ramen, rice dishes, and other Izakaya—essentially Japanese bar food. It would be impossible to pick anything here that isn't exceptional.

2 BIG JOHN'S TAVERN

Done with the only sushi visit in the book, we make our way down Bay Street to the right. Across the street on your left is a grocery store, Harris Teeter—a good stop to grab something you may have forgotten at non-convenient store prices. Even a bottle of water for your stroll. A few blocks up you will approach the City Market part of town. Before you do, on your right (assuming it's after 4 p.m.) you will find **BIG JOHN'S TAVERN**. A lively place with a colorful history.

Although Big John's opened in 1955, it is considered one of the oldest bars in Charleston. After a fire in 2015, Big John's finally closed. Then it reopened as another bar, which lasted about 5 years. In 2020, three locals looked into buying the building and bringing back Big John's. Boy did they ever!

It's certainly not what it was, but it is now a beautiful space with great food and a stellar beer selection. The menu is diverse (duck nachos or a Chicago dog?) and the atmosphere is great. Ask them about their speakeasy, a room you will need a reservation to enter.

Charleston's Bay Street is home to a passenger Cruise Ship Terminal. While Carnival Cruise Lines is only cruise line to call this port home, two others (American and Silversea) also stop in Charleston. A popular route from Charleston is a six-day cruise to and from Bermuda.

3

RUDY ROYALE

Leaving Big John's, continue down Bay Street. On your right you will cross Charleston's City Market area on your way south. Before you get to the next corner, you will come to our next stop, **RUDY ROYALE**.

This place is known for chicken and cocktails. You'll also find shareable comfort food classics like deviled eggs, fried oysters, fried pickles, and cornbread.

The go-to here? The Notorious Chicken Sandwich topped with pimiento cheese, slaw, and pickles. There are also entrees as well, but with a chicken sandwich like this . . . ? As soon as you see one . . . you will understand. Save room for dessert on our next stop, though.

4

CARMELLA'S CAFÉ AND DESSERT BAR

Our next stop is directly across the street from the front door of Rudy Royale. **CARMELLA'S** is a classic Charleston downtown dessert spot. I don't know that I have ever seen a time when Carmella's wasn't busy. It doesn't matter the time of day. Midday snack or quick bite for lunch or after dinner sweets, this Italian café is exceptional.

The cannoli cake is a regular crowd pleaser, but don't overlook the chocolate peanut butter cake with peanut butter and honey filling.

The list of coffee offerings is extensive as are their Drunken Milkshakes. There's a nice glass of wine list as well as a wonderful selection of gelato and sorbetto. Does this sound like a one-stop-shop? It most certainly is.

TIP

You should plan this crawl with enough time to enjoy the Southern extreme of Bay Street at the Battery. It offers sweeping views of the Harbor. In the distance is Fort Sumter, which was involved in the beginning of the Civil War.

5

THE GRIFFON

Exiting Carmella's and turning left to continue down Bay Street, you will see a flurry of some of the area's most classic restaurants. Slightly North of Broad (S.N.O.B.), Magnolia's, High Cotton, and the Gin Joint have all achieved legendary status around these parts. They are all worthy of your attention for a proper dinner if you are looking for one. Except for the Gin Joint, which is a classic cocktail bar with proper snacks and a couple of sandwiches. Any way you slice it, they are all good. If the Gin Joint opened during the midday, they would have been a stop. Something to definitely keep in mind.

Continue down Bay to the corner of Vendue Range, at which point you will turn left and go about a half block to our final stop, **THE GRIFFON**.

Southern Living Magazine referred to the Griffon as one of the best bars in the South. A well-deserved honor. Not to be confused with a classic dive bar, the Griffon bills itself as Charleston's Best Pub. Traditional bar food

is what you will find. Nachos, wings, fried this or that, plus a few salads. Burgers, sandwiches, and fry baskets.

The beer list is extensive and impressive. There is a full liquor bar as well. The walls are a sight we've all seen before, with autographed dollar bills. It's a great spot made popular not only because of the food and drink but also because of its proximity to two of Charleston's most popular landmarks.

Joe Riley Waterfront Park sits about 60 paces from the front of the Griffon. Another 200 or so paces, and you will see Charleston's famed pineapple fountain. If you walk to the end of Waterfront Park and turn right up North Adgers Wharf (a street), you will find Rainbow Row, arguably Charleston's most photographed stretch of homes.

THE BROAD STREET CRAWL

1. **MILLERS ALL DAY,** 120 KING STREET, CHARLESTON, (843) 501-7342, MILLERSALLDAY.COM

2. **GAULART & MALICLET (FAST AND FRENCH),** 98 BROAD STREET, CHARLESTON, (843) 577-9797, FASTANDFRENCHCHARLESTON.COM

3. **BROWN DOG DELI,** 40 BROAD STREET, CHARLESTON, (843) 853-8081, BROWNDOGDELI.COM

4. **BLIND TIGER PUB,** 36-38 BROAD STREET, CHARLESTON, (843) 872-6700, BLINDTIGERCHS.COM

5. **BRASSERIE LA BANQUE/OAK STEAKHOUSE,** 1 BROAD STREET, CHARLESTON, (843) 779-1800, BRASSERIELABANQUE.COM

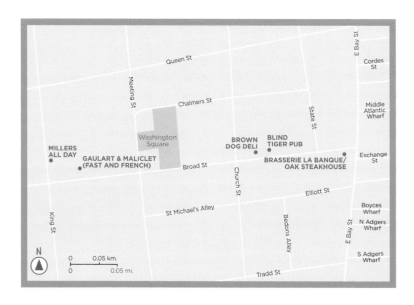

Broad Street

Charleston's Original Main Street Crawl

The history along this several block stretch is far more significant than you may realize at first glance. To the north, you find the whole of the Charleston Peninsula. To the south, you find a largely residential neighborhood known as the Battery, Charleston's most exclusive neighborhood. In between is Broad Street, a center of city business and banking dotted with both casual and fine dining eateries good enough to offer an attorney a quick lunch between sessions or a banker a high-end meal with a new client. But we start with breakfast.

1

MILLERS ALL DAY

Breakfast is, after all, the most important meal of the day, right? That being said, our Broad Street Crawl actually begins around the corner on King Street. About 50 feet north of Broad at **MILLERS ALL DAY**.

Contrary to its name, Millers All Day closes mid-afternoon. But don't hold that against them; they get going early with an impressive selection of breakfast classics. Biscuits and gravy, pancakes, steak and eggs, and most things in between. It is very popular with a younger crowd looking to properly manage that hangover. On the healthy side, you can find soups, yogurt bowls, and more. But make no mistake, one of the showstoppers here is the hot honey chicken bacon egg and cheese biscuit. The other is a hot honey donut with house honey and peach preserves. Are you getting the picture? One other thing: don't pass on the grits.

2 GAULART & MALICLET (FAST AND FRENCH)

This place is fascinating. It opened in 1984 as a tiny café offering classic bites from France. It became very popular in part because of its proximity to the upscale neighborhood across the street (the Battery) plus the business crowd that spends a lot of its time here during the week.

When I first visited in 2012, I loved it. Even though I couldn't pronounce its name no matter how hard I tried. The next time I visited, someone had given it a "fast and French" moniker. Clearly, I wasn't alone because now everyone knows where it is.

Fast and French is just that. Breakfast, lunch, or dinner. Croques and other sandwiches, salads, mimosas, coffees. By night you can find some classic dishes like Chicken Normandy or Provençal. This is every bit French and, yes, it is fast, which makes it quite popular during the week for business lunches. This is a must stop in Charleston. And I still don't know how to pronounce their proper name.

LUNCH AL FRESCO

In between our stops at Millers All Day and Gaulart & Maliclet you will find Washington Square Park, a city square that dates back to 1818. It was named for George Washington in 1881 at the Centennial of the surrender at Yorktown. It is one of the quieter spots to enjoy a sandwich in the shade in the city.

3 BROWN DOG DELI

Our next stop on the crawl isn't for a couple of blocks. But between here and there, there is more than enough history to keep you busy. Continuing up Broad, you will come to the corner of Meeting Street. Charleston's Historic Courthouse sits at this intersection. You might want to check out the museum there.

A couple of blocks ahead, you will find the **BROWN DOG DELI**. Another fast but good lunch spot for business folks on the go.

This is one of two locations of this classic deli in Charleston, the second located not all that far away on Calhoun Street. That will give you an idea of how popular they are. Sandwiches and salads much like you would find in any deli are the norm here—with a twist. Southern, of course.

For example, there's Pig and Fig: pulled pork, fig rosemary preserves, cheddar, and Granny Smith apple. That should get your attention!

Vegetarian options include Impossible burgers and the very popular Chic Feel Ay (any guess what that is a knock off of)?

4

BLIND TIGER PUB

Next door is a historic pub called **BLIND TIGER PUB**. The name has a significant place in this city's history. "Blind Tigers" were a nickname given to places that sold alcoholic beverages illegally. They were also known as Blind Pigs. More commonly, they were speakeasies. It is believed that this spot on Broad Street was one such place.

These days, the beer flows very legally. It is the most casual pub on Broad Street and thus very popular at all hours. The beer garden in back is also a significant draw when the weather isn't too oppressive.

The scene is inviting, with televisions carrying sporting events all around. It's a good stop for a pint and perhaps some oysters—they offer fried, but raw is the way to go on the Carolina coast.

DRAFTING A CONSTITUTION

The John Rutledge House (at 116 Broad Street) is home to a second-floor drawing room where several drafts of the U.S. Constitution were written. The homeowner, John Rutledge, not only signed the Constitution but was also South Carolina's first and only president (so far).

5 OAK STEAKHOUSE/BRASSERIE LA BANQUE

Our final stops—plural—on this crawl aren't really stops at all unless it is after 5 p.m. As I've said, some of Charleston's best eats can be found at the dinner hour. Well, sitting at the end of Broad near Bay Street are two fine establishments owned by the same group and worthy of a mention here.

OAK STEAKHOUSE and **BRASSERIE LA BANQUE** offer different experiences. Some locals will tell you they believe Oak is the best steakhouse in the city. That usually gets a scrunched nose from the Hall's Chophouse faithful, but regardless. They are both exceptional.

Meanwhile, the Brasserie is classic French and fun with a great wine list. It is as inviting for a quick glass of wine at the bar (if you can get a seat) or a fully seated dinner.

Outside and across the street meanwhile is one final landmark. The Tavern at Rainbow Row is America's oldest package store, serving Charleston since 1686. So-called modern law prohibits spirits from being sold in the same place as beer and wine so there's a wall dividing them.

THE PARC CIRCLE CRAWL

1. **HOLY CITY BREWING,** 1021 ARAGON AVENUE, NORTH CHARLESTON, (843) 459-2948, HOLYCITYBREWING.COM

2. **JACKRABBIT FILLY,** 4628 SPRUILL AVENUE, NORTH CHARLESTON, (843) 460-0037, JACKRABBITFILLY.COM

3. **EVO (EXTRA VIRGIN OVEN),** 1075 E. MONTAGUE AVENUE, NORTH CHARLESTON, (843) 225-1796, EVOPIZZA.COM

4. **PADDOCK & WHISKY,** 1074 E. MONTAGUE AVENUE, NORTH CHARLESTON, (843) 203-4238, PADDOCKANDWHISKY.COM

5. **THE TATTOOED MOOSE,** 4845 CHATEAU AVENUE, NORTH CHARLESTON, (843) 277-2990, TATTOOEDMOOSE.COM

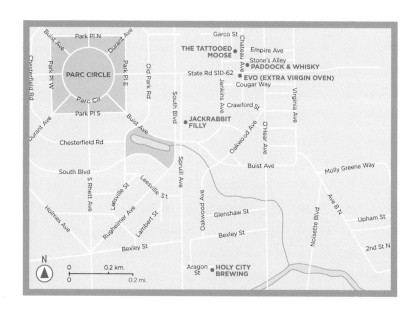

Parc Circle

A Modern Culinary Suburb

Perhaps the most mentioned section of Charleston's culinary scene during the extensive research for this book, Parc Circle has become a culinary hub all on its own.

Located roughly 10 miles north of the heart of the Charleston Peninsula, it is technically the City of North Charleston. Parc Circle was designed in 1912. More recently, it has seen a dramatic influx of creative minds, culinary and otherwise, looking for something different (and very likely less expensive) than the more developed sections of the peninsula to the south.

As a result, this is some of the best casual food in the area dedicated almost exclusively to locals. If you know, you know. And the ones who do? They swear by it. If you are coming to Charleston specifically to eat and you'd like to get a true local slice of life, Parc Circle is worth a visit.

1

HOLY CITY BREWING

One trip to this section of Charleston and you will see that HOLY CITY is hardly the only brewery in the area. If you put pen to paper, you could probably come up with over a dozen in this neighborhood alone. Holy City, however, delivers solid eats to go along with their more than extensive list of beers. Burgers and sandwiches, salads and sides. A little bit of something for everyone. With both indoor and outdoor seating.

While it may not look like it, **Parc Circle** is technically North Charleston's Historic District. It was originally settled in 1898 and officially founded in 1912 as Garden City. The area served as a neighborhood for modest single-family homes for workers at the area's factories and nearby naval base.

JACKRABBIT FILLY

JACKRABBIT FILLY is a classic case of food truck gone so wild that they turned it into a brick-and-mortar location and haven't looked back. The cuisine is a unique blend of Chinese and American comfort foods, with menu items like Buffalo Krab Rangoon Dip and Karaage (Japanese fried chicken) with lemon mayo, ponzu, and togarashi.

This might be the most popular restaurant in the Parc Circle. Food is served family-style, and sharing is encouraged. Reservations are required, and there will be a charge to your credit card if you no-show. Yes, this is a friendly and inviting space, but they are popular enough to demand that. It is outstanding. On Sundays they offer a dim sum brunch.

3 EVO (EXTRA VIRGIN OVEN)

If Jackrabbit Filly is Parc Circle's most popular restaurant, EVO is likely its most popular pizzeria and for very good reason. It's delicious.

EVO opened after a couple of years of operating a pizza food truck. They developed a following almost immediately—one that very much exists today. If they are open for business, the room is very likely full and the pies are flying in and out of their wood-fired oven. There are also salads and sandwiches. When you sell bumper stickers that read Pork Trifecta, you know the pie is popular. Topped with red sauce, house made sausage, pepperoni, bacon, and parmigiano Reggiano, how can it not be? The pies are smallish, but definitely good enough for two to split. Especially if you have other stops on your crawl.

4

PADDOCK & WHISKY

Almost across the street (as most everything is along this stretch) from EVO, you will find another somewhat unique spot. Certainly not unique in a Southern sense, but unique for this part of town. Paddock & Whisky.

Located in a converted bank building (a newer bank, not an old historic one), **PADDOCK & WHISKY** offers a healthy selection of bourbons and whiskeys. If you can schedule a tasting in advance and the name of your restaurant says "Whiskey," you know they take them seriously.

They offer dinner during the week, lunch on Fridays and brunch on weekends. There's an eye-popping chicken sandwich—you know, breast larger than the bun, dripping with pimento cheese—the kind of sandwich that creates a wave of them once the first one makes its way through the dining room.

Parc Circle—and more generally, North Charleston—is home to no less than a dozen breweries and distilleries. Only a few are within walking distance of each other, but the neighborhood as a whole is a welcome scene for beer enthusiasts who enjoy a taprooms crawl.

THE TATTOOED MOOSE

Once upon a time "down the neck" of the peninsula as they say, **THE TATTOOED MOOSE** was the stuff of legends. Built into an old shack but offering some of the most delicious and creative comfort foods around, they developed one of the more loyal followings in town.

That is still the case, but gentrification and development sometimes has a way of making things better, depending on who you ask. The Moose expanded a few years ago and in doing so moved away from their original location up to this area in North Charleston. They have more space that they undoubtedly appreciate and their guests have more space for parking, which we very much appreciate.

The duck fat fries served with garlic aioli are the flagship bite here, but it is all good. Philly cheesesteak egg rolls? Short rib chili? You get the idea; this is serious stick-to-your-ribs food. Although there are a few salads, this isn't a place to worry about your diet. Check out the Thanksgiving sammy. Or Porkstrami Reuben. Or boozy adult floats. Or burgers. Or Morrocan gyro. Get it yet? Do it.

The "Best of the Rest" Appendix

Like I said, there is no way to do it all. Eat it all or crawl it all. There will always be more, including these, many of which are dinner only and one that is a beautiful 20–30-minute drive out to the beach at Sullivan's Island—Obstinate Daughter.

LISTED ALPHABETICALLY

BASIC KITCHEN
82 Wentworth Street, Charleston, 29401, (843) 789-4568, basickitchen.com

BIG BAD BREAKFAST
456 Meeting Street, Charleston, 29401, (843) 459-1800, bigbadbreakfast .com

CHUBBY FISH
252 Coming Street, Charleston, 29403, (843) 222-3949, chubbyfish charleston.com

ESTADIO
122 Spring Street, Charleston, 29403, (843) 793-1029, estadio-chs.com

FIG
232 Meeting Street, Charleston, 29401, (843) 805-5900, eatatfig.com

HANNIBAL'S KITCHEN
16 Blake Street, Charleston, 29403, (843) 722-2256, hannibalkitchen.com

LA FARFALLE
15 Beaufain Street, Charleston, 29401, (843) 212-0920, lefarfallecharleston .com

OBSTINATE DAUGHTER
2063 Middle Street, Sullivan's Island, 29482, theobstinatedaughter.com

SNOB
192 East Bay Street, Charleston, 29401, (843) 723-3424, snobcharleston .com

VERN'S
41 Bogard Street, Charleston, 29403, vernschs.com (reservations via Resy)

Rooftop Appendix

We had fun with this one, counting all of the rooftops and trying to make them a crawl of their own. Ultimately, they are too far apart and really too incredibly diverse to make into a crawl. But they cannot be ignored. They offer great vibes across the board and some of them are must-stops if you like rooftop vibes.

LISTED ALPHABETICALLY

AQUA TERRACE AT CHARLESTON MARRIOTT
170 Lockwood Drive, Charleston, 29403, (843) 723-3000, aquaterrace charleston.com

THE CITRUS CLUB AT THE DEWBERRY HOTEL
334 Meeting Street, Charleston 29403, (843) 558-8000, thedewberry charleston.com

THE COCKTAIL CLUB
479 King Street, Charleston, 29403, (843) 724-9411, thecocktailclub charleston.com

ÉLEVÉ AT GRAND BOHEMIAN HOTEL
55 Wentworth Street, Charleston 29401, (843) 724-4144, elevecharleston .com

FIAT LUX AT HOTEL BENNETT
404 King Street, Charleston, 29403, (843) 313-1798, hotelbennett.com

INK ROOFTOP AND LOUNGE
565 King Street, Charleston, 29403, (843) 501-7220, inkcharleston.com

LOUTREL ROOFTOP TERRACE
61 State Street, Charleston, 29403, (843) 872-9600, theloutrel.com

PAVILION BAR AT PAVILION HOTEL
225 E. Bay Street, Charleston, 29401, (843) 723-0500, marketpavilion.com

POUR TAPROOM
560 King Street, Charleston, 29403, (843) 414-4900, pourtaproomcharles-ton.com

REVELRY BREWING AND ROOFTOP
10 Conroy Street, Charleston, 29403, (843) 376-1303, revelrybrewingco .com

THE ROOFTOP AT VENDUE
19 Vendue Range, Charleston, 29401, (843) 577-7970, thevendue.com

STARS ROOFTOP AND GRILL
495 King Street, Charleston, 29401, (843) 577-0100, starsrestaurant.com

UPTOWN SOCIAL
587 King Street, Charleston, 29403, (843) 793-1837, uptownsocialsc.com

THE WATCH ROOFTOP KITCHEN
75 Wentworth Street, Charleston, 29401, (843) 518-5115, thewatchcharleston
.com

Photo Credits

All photos by Jesse Blanco except for the following:

Photos on pages viii–ix, 10–11, 22–23, 36–37, 50–51, 64–65, 80–81, 94–95,
   108–109, 122, and 124: Courtesy of Explore Charleston
167 Sushi: Provided by 167 Sushi
Bin 152: Provided by Bin 152
Blind Tiger Pub: Provided Blind Tiger Pub
Bodega CHS: Provided by Bodega CHS
Brasserie La Banque: Provided by Brasserie LaBanque
Brown Dog Deli: Provided by Brown Dog Deli
Butcher and Bee: Photos by Andrew Cebulka
Callie's Hot Little Biscuit: Provided by Callie's Hot Little Biscuit
Chocolate by Adam Turoni: Provided by Chocolate by Adam
Church and Union: Provided by C&U
Clarkes Coffee: Provided by Lindsay Shorter and Hotel Emeline
Fast and French: Provided by Fast and French
Holy City Brewing: Provided by Holy City Brewing
Jack Rabbit Filly: Provided by Jack Rabbit Filly
Malagón: Duck photo provided by Malagó
Millers All Day: Provided by Millers All Day
Neon Tiger: Provided by Neon Tiger
Prohibition: Provided by Prohibition (except the wings, which Jesse Blanco
   claims)
Rancho Lewis: Provided by Rancho Lewis
Rodney Scott BBQ: Provided by Rodney Scott BBQ
Rudy Royale: Provided by Rudy Royale
The Pass: Provided by The Pass
Royal American: Provided by Royal American
The Tattooed Moose: Provided by The Tattooed Moose

Index

167 Sushi, 82

Benne's at Peninsula Grill, 69
Big John's Tavern, 85
Bin 152 Wine Shop, 60
Blind Tiger Pub, 102
Bodega CHS, 44
Brasserie La Banque, 104
Brown Dog Deli, 100
Byrd Cookie Company, 74

Callie's Hot Little Biscuit, 42
Carmella's Café and Dessert Bar, 88
Caviar & Bananas Gourmet Market and Café, 52
Chocolat by Adam Turoni, 58
Church and Union Charleston, 72
Clerks Coffee Company at Hotel Emeline, 70

Edmonds Oast Brewing Company, 2
Extra Virgin Oven (EVO), 115

Félix, 38

Gaulart & Maliclet, 98
Goat, Sheep, Cow, North, 4
Griffon, The, 90

Holy City Brewing, 110
Home Team BBQ, 5
Hyman's Seafood, 66

Jackrabbit Filly, 112

La Patisserie, 46
Leon's, 18
Lewis BBQ, 6
Little Jack's Tavern, 16

Malagón Mercado and Tapería, 31
Millers All Day, 96

Neon Tiger, 21

Oak Steakhouse, 104
Off Track Ice Cream, 54
Ordinary, The, 41

Paddock & Whisky, 116
Pass Sandwich Shop, The, 29
Pink Cactus Mexican, 28
Port of Call Food Court and Brew Hall, 76

Rancho Lewis, 2
Raw 167 Oyster Bar, 56
Recovery Room, The, 20
Rodney Scott's Whole Hog BBQ, 14
Royal American, The, 8

Tattooed Moose, The, 118

Xiao Bao Biscuit, 26

Acknowledgments

In the summer of 2022, I completed what I thought at the time was one of the more challenging assignments I had ever been given. I had written my first book, *Savannah Food Crawls*. I was over the moon. A few months later the call came asking if I'd be interested in taking on Charleston's food scene. Uh, yeah? I guess so.

Taking on one of the most celebrated food scenes in America was most certainly intimidating. I told myself I would take on this project the same way I would eat an elephant. One bite at a time. It may look "fun" and/or "sexy" from the outside, but don't get it twisted. This is a lot of work. Work I could never in a million lifetimes get done by myself.

The list of people and characters who have helped—and many times carried us—along the way would be long enough to fill a novel. I wish I could say I don't know where to begin to say thank you, but I most certainly do.

My becoming a food writer was Senea Crystal's idea. She not only planted the seed back in 2010, but was critical to the brand's creation and initial growth. None of this would have been possible without her vision and passion to help make it happen.

To my dear friend Monique Cabrera, who was calling shots on this journey 5-plus years in advance. I was better prepared to handle life as an entrepreneur because of that. It's been so critical. Thank you. Also, to my friends Michael Owens and Joe Marinelli for the crutch as we limped along trying to make sense of it all.

A huge thank-you to everyone at Globe Pequot for the faith and trust to document Charleston's food scene for you.

To my tribe: Tara Parker, Lauren Dasher Blanco, Amanda Cifaldi, Dawn Harris, Jennifer Wielgoszinski, and my sister Sandy. I'm probably still bumping into walls without your unwavering support.

Finally and most importantly, of course, to my beautiful wife Sheila and daughter Alexandra. There aren't enough thank-yous to share for your allowing me to pursue a dream. You are both my entire world and I am nothing without your love and support. At least you get to eat well, right?

About the Author

JESSE BLANCO is a Savannah-based food writer and television show host. His culinary journey has taken across the South in search of great food and interesting people. There are never too many visits to Charleston, especially when food is involved. He's always up for a road trip.